Auto Body 30 Day 5S Action Log

Start Date:____________________ Work Area:____________________

Date Logged	Item Number	5S Problem	Suggestion to Solve Problem	Who is Responsible

Auto Body 30 Day 5S Action Log

Start Date:____________________ Work Area:____________________

Date Logged	Item Number	5S Problem	Suggestion to Solve Problem	Who is Responsible

Auto Body 30 Day 5S Action Log

Start Date:____________________ Work Area:____________________

Date Logged	Item Number	5S Problem	Suggestion to Solve Problem	Who is Responsible

Auto Body

30 Day 5S Action Log

Start Date:____________________ Work Area:____________________

Date Logged	Item Number	5S Problem	Suggestion to Solve Problem	Who is Responsible

Auto Body 30 Day 5S Action Log

Start Date:____________________ Work Area:____________________

Date Logged	Item Number	5S Problem	Suggestion to Solve Problem	Who is Responsible

Auto Body 30 Day 5S Action Log

Start Date:____________________ Work Area:____________________

Date Logged	Item Number	5S Problem	Suggestion to Solve Problem	Who is Responsible

Auto Body 30 Day 5S Action Log

Start Date:____________________ Work Area:____________________

Date Logged	Item Number	5S Problem	Suggestion to Solve Problem	Who is Responsible

Auto Body 30 Day 5S Action Log

Start Date:____________________ Work Area:____________________

Date Logged	Item Number	5S Problem	Suggestion to Solve Problem	Who is Responsible

Auto Body

30 Day 5S Action Log

Start Date:__________ __________ Work Area:____________________

Date Logged	Item Number	5S Problem	Suggestion to Solve Problem	Who is Responsible

Auto Body 30 Day 5S Action Log

Start Date:____________________ Work Area:____________________

Date Logged	Item Number	5S Problem	Suggestion to Solve Problem	Who is Responsible

Auto Body 30 Day 5S Action Log

Start Date: ____________________ Work Area: ____________________

Date Logged	Item Number	5S Problem	Suggestion to Solve Problem	Who is Responsible

Auto Body

30 Day 5S Action Log

Start Date:____________________ Work Area:_____________________

Date Logged	Item Number	5S Problem	Suggestion to Solve Problem	Who is Responsible

Auto Body

30 Day 5S Action Log

Start Date:____________________ Work Area:____________________

Date Logged	Item Number	5S Problem	Suggestion to Solve Problem	Who is Responsible

Auto Body 30 Day 5S Action Log

Start Date:____________________ Work Area:____________________

Date Logged	Item Number	5S Problem	Suggestion to Solve Problem	Who is Responsible

Auto Body

30 Day 5S Action Log

Start Date:____________________ Work Area:____________________

Date Logged	Item Number	5S Problem	Suggestion to Solve Problem	Who is Responsible

Auto Body 30 Day 5S Action Log

Start Date: ____________________ Work Area: ____________________

Date Logged	Item Number	5S Problem	Suggestion to Solve Problem	Who is Responsible

Auto Body 30 Day 5S Action Log

Start Date:____________________ Work Area:____________________

Date Logged	Item Number	5S Problem	Suggestion to Solve Problem	Who is Responsible

Auto Body 30 Day 5S Action Log

Start Date:______________________ Work Area:______________________

Date Logged	Item Number	5S Problem	Suggestion to Solve Problem	Who is Responsible

Auto Body 30 Day 5S Action Log

Start Date:____________________ Work Area:____________________

Date Logged	Item Number	5S Problem	Suggestion to Solve Problem	Who is Responsible

Auto Body 30 Day 5S Action Log

Start Date:____________________ Work Area:____________________

Date Logged	Item Number	5S Problem	Suggestion to Solve Problem	Who is Responsible

Auto Body 30 Day 5S Action Log

Start Date:____________________ Work Area:______________________

Date Logged	Item Number	5S Problem	Suggestion to Solve Problem	Who is Responsible

Auto Body 30 Day 5S Action Log

Start Date:____________________ Work Area:_____________________

Date Logged	Item Number	5S Problem	Suggestion to Solve Problem	Who is Responsible

Auto Body 30 Day 5S Action Log

Start Date:______________________ Work Area:______________________

Date Logged	Item Number	5S Problem	Suggestion to Solve Problem	Who is Responsible

Auto Body 30 Day 5S Action Log

Start Date:____________________ Work Area:____________________

Date Logged	Item Number	5S Problem	Suggestion to Solve Problem	Who is Responsible

Auto Body

30 Day 5S Action Log

Start Date:____________________ Work Area:____________________

Date Logged	Item Number	5S Problem	Suggestion to Solve Problem	Who is Responsible